The Future of Fashion

How Sustainable Innovations are Transforming the Industry

Table of Contents

Chapter 1. Introduction

Immerse yourself in the vibrant, evolving world of fashion with our special report, "The Future of Fashion: How Sustainable Innovations are Transforming the Industry". As the industry grapples with its own environmental footprint, innovators rise to the occasion, creating a sartorial revolution. This comprehensive report unearths the cutting-edge techniques being utilised, from recyclable fabrics to zero-waste design, and ferries you through a journey of transformation. Both revolutionary and tantalizingly fashionable, this report resonates with those who believe in a future where style and sustainability go hand in hand. Your runway to understanding the glorious amalgamation of fashion and ecology starts here. Jump into this whirlwind of change and let's build a seasonless, sustainable, and stylish future together. Buy the report today and be part of fashion's green revolution.

Chapter 2. The Climate Crisis and Fashion: An Inevitable Intersection

It's a truth universally acknowledged that the fashion industry, responsible for 8 to 10 percent of global carbon emissions, higher than all international flights and maritime shipping combined, has a significant impact on the environment. The domino effects of climate change have become too significant to ignore, making it imperative for the realm of fashion to intersect with environmental responsibility. This inescapable intersection forms the basis for sweeping changes and innovations within the industry, as we look towards a sustainable and fashion-forward future.

2.1. The Environmental Impact of the Fashion Industry

The fashion industry has traditionally been intrinsically linked with environmental degradation. From the utilization of massive quantities of water in textile production, to deforestation associated with fabric cultivation, to the vast carbon emissions resulting from global shipping and manufacturing, the effects are widespread and devastating. Additionally, the highly consumer-driven nature of the industry, propelled by fast-fashion trends, results in a significant waste production. As clothing quickly moves in and out of style, cast-off items pile up in landfills, making fashion the second largest polluter of fresh water globally.

2.2. A Rendezvous with Reality: The Wake-Up Call

The stark reality of climate change ushered a crucial wake-up call to the industry. Increasingly frequent and severe weather events, water shortages, and shifting agriculture patterns not only threaten natural ecosystems but also the very resources that the fashion industry depends upon - cotton, leather, and clean water. Thus, industry stakeholders have started to recognize the significance of sustainability, not just as a marketing strategy, but as a fundamental business requisite. This rendezvous with reality has initiated a shift towards practices that lessen environmental harm and promote sustainability.

2.3. Rise of Eco-Fashion: Meeting at the Intersection

In response to the environmental crisis at hand, the fashion industry began embracing 'Eco-fashion'. This integrated approach employs techniques such as the use of organic, recycled, or biodegradable materials, along with ethically sourced, fair trade labor. Brands have also started to prioritize durability, aiming to extend the lifespan of their products and deter the wastefulness often associated with fast fashion. Major players and start-ups alike have been revamping their methodologies, driven by both a moral obligation towards Earth and a demand from a climate-aware clientele.

2.4. Sustainable Apparel's Bid to Lessen Water Consumption

Water usage constitutes one of the most pressing environmental issues tied to the fashion industry. It takes a heavy toll on the availability of a precious resource. As such, innovative techniques to lessen water consumption substantially have surged. From tanning leather using rhubarb extracts instead of water-intensive chromium salts, to using digital printing for dyeing to reduce water usage by 50 percent, the industry seeks to renew its relationship with water.

2.5. The Zero-Waste Design Principle

Zero-waste design serves as one of the transformative strategies uniting fashion and environmental consciousness. This principle asserts that waste should not be a by-product of apparel production. Designers, guided by this approach, manipulate patterns in the design phase to utilize every piece of fabric, leaving little to no textile waste. The future of this approach hinges upon technological advancements that can make it a normative practice across the industry, democratizing access to sustainable fashion.

2.6. Circular Fashion: The Industry's Lifeline

Circular fashion, characterized by an intentional, sustainable, and circular lifecycle for each piece of clothing, represents another pivotal point of intersection between fashion and the environment. This methodology seeks to ensure that materials used in production are biodegradable or recycled while respecting ethical labor standards. Embracing rental fashion, second-hand clothing, upcycling, and recycling garments – these are all facets of the circular fashion movement.

In the spirit of true circularity, some companies have initiated take-back programs to accept used products from customers. Once returned, these materials are recycled or upcycled, creating a closed-loop, reducing waste, and lessening the need for new resource extraction.

2.7. The Road Ahead: Policy, Technology, and Consumer Power

The road to sustainability is multifaceted, requiring cohesive effort from policy makers, fashion houses, technologists, and consumers. Stringent regulatory frameworks are essential to hold the industry accountable for its environmental footprint. Simultaneously, continuing technological advancements can further propel sustainable practices. Moreover, empowered consumers play a crucial role in dictating market trends towards eco-friendly products.

The confluence of the fashion industry with climate change is a challenge that can only be overcome by acknowledging the intertwining of the two. Modern fashion's spirit aspires towards sustainability, marrying style and environmental consciousness. This shift is not simply inevitable but also desirable for a truly fashionable and responsible world.

Chapter 3. Sustainability: The New Black in Fashion

Sustainability in the fashion industry has emerged as a pressing issue. Recognizing the significant costs that fast fashion inflicts upon the environment, major players in the industry are now harnessing innovative techniques and materials to mitigate their ecological footprint. As we delve into the intricacies of this transition, we uncover a plethora of initiatives and advancements that not only illustrate the new trajectory of fashion but also chart a course for its sustainable future.

3.1. Sustainable Fabrics: The Materials of the Future

Foremost among these innovations is the development and use of sustainable fabrics. A significant proportion of the industry's environmental impact stems from the cultivation, extraction, and processing of raw materials. Traditional fabrics such as cotton, silk, and wool place a considerable burden on the environment due to their intensive cultivation processes involving pesticide use and water wastage.

To counter this, fashion houses and manufacturers are increasingly turning to alternatives. These include organic cotton, which reduces pesticide use, and regenerative wool, which incorporates land management techniques that not only reduce harm but also actively restore ecosystems.

Materials science is pushing the boundaries with the introduction of fabrics derived from unconventional but sustainable sources. These include fabrics made from recycled plastic bottles, pineapple leaves, coffee grounds, and even mushrooms. These efforts reflect a concerted move towards circular fashion, particularly in their utilization of waste to produce usable garments.

3.2. Zero-Waste Design: Cutting out the Excess

Zero-waste design is another significant leap towards sustainability. Traditional fashion practices generate massive amounts of waste at the cutting stage, with up to 15% of fabric ending up as scraps. Zero-waste design presents a fresh take on garment construction that eliminates waste from the cutting process.

The process revolutionizes traditional patterns, using innovative layout strategies and modular designs to ensure that every part of the fabric is used. Several designers have embraced this philosophy, and their collections illuminate a vision of fashion where sophistication does not come at the expense of sustainability.

3.3. Fashion Technology: Forward-thinking Innovation

Technology is a strong ally in fashion's march towards sustainability. Predictive modeling enables manufacturers to produce only what is necessary, cutting down overproduction. Meanwhile, new technologies that use waterless dyeing methods offer colour without the environmental costs traditionally associated with this process.

Another groundbreaking innovation is the use of 3D design tools, which facilitates waste reduction and encourages circularity. They allow designers to visualize their creations and make necessary adjustments without first producing a physical prototype, thereby saving materials.

Additionally, blockchain technology furnishes transparency in supply chains, making it easier for consumers to make informed choices and for companies to trace their products from raw material to finished garment.

3.4. The Role of Consumer Awareness

Consumer awareness is a significant driver of sustainability in the fashion industry. Buyers are becoming increasingly conscious of the environmental impact of their purchases and are actively seeking brands that align with their values.

The fashion industry has seen a surge in demand for sustainable products, with many consumers willing to pay a premium for ethically produced apparel. This has put pressure on brands to reassess their practices and place sustainability at the forefront of their strategies. Mobile apps and traceability platforms play a crucial role by providing consumers with information about the sustainability credentials of their purchases.

3.5. The Road Ahead: Successfully Merging Style with Sustainability

The fashion industry's future is centred on striking a balance between producing stylish, desirable garments and respecting the environment. The amalgamation of innovative techniques and materials, responsible consumer behavior, and forward-thinking policies will shape the trajectory of the industry.

While remarkable progress has been made, there remain hurdles to be overcome, including scaling sustainable practices, dealing with industry inertia, and refining regulations. However, if the industry continues on its current path, it promises to transform fashion into an enterprise that epitomizes style, function, and sustainability.

The future of fashion is not just about the garments we wear, but the processes and ethos that create them. By embracing these changes and nurturing the innovations they bring, we will cultivate an industry that is truly sustainable, creating a wardrobe that reflects not just our individual style, but our collective ethos of care for our environment.

Chapter 4. Understanding the Impact of Conscious Consumerism

The genesis of conscious consumerism can be traced back to growing public awareness about the ecological implications of their buying habits. Increasingly, consumers are pushing back against the industry's traditional make-use-dispose model, demanding more ecological responsibility from manufacturers and designers.

4.1. The Rise of Conscious Consumerism

Studies show that the concept of conscious consumerism has gained traction around the globe. Customers are considering the environmental footprint of their purchases more than ever before, thus forcing the fashion industry to reckon with their practices. A study by Nielsen suggests that nearly three-quarters of Millennials and Gen Z are willing to pay more for sustainable products. This substantial shift in consumer purchasing habits cannot be ignored by the industry; instead, it needs to adapt to accommodate this sweeping change.

4.2. The Power of the Green Dollar

In today's market-driven world, consumers have immense power with their spending choices — a power that more are harnessing to make companies consider their environmental and social impact. Sustainability efforts are increasingly being woven into corporate missions, to attract the green dollar. This is a win-win because it helps businesses improve their bottom line while alsomaking a positive impact on the planet.

The green dollar is literally compelling the fashion industry to seek sustainability. Brands that disregard this change risk tarnishing their reputation and consequently, their revenues. Conscious consumers not only want to purchase eco-friendly products; they want to know how they are made and who makes them. They demand transparency that spans the entire supply chain.

4.3. The Emergence of Slow Fashion

One direct consequence of conscious consumerism is the emergence and increased acceptance of slow fashion. This philosophy eschews the fast, cheap, and disposable model in favor of one that values quality, longevity, and fair treatment of workers.

Slow fashion encourages consumers to buy fewer items but choose those that last longer, are ethically produced, and have minimal environmental impact. It also promotes recycling and reuse to extend the life of garments while also reducing the demand for new materials.

4.4. Conscious Consumption and Its Impact on Industry Practices

The rise of conscious consumerism has pushed the industry towards a more sustainable path, prompting changes inproduction processes. Brands are now investing more in research and development to produce textiles that are less environmentally damaging. They are using natural, recycled, or biodegradable materials and minimizing or eliminating the use of harmful chemicals. Brands are also focusing on waste reduction during manufacturing and optimizing energy consumption.

4.5. Working Conditions and Workers' Rights

Conscious consumers aren't just concerned about the environment; they care about the people who make their clothes. Brands are now compelled to be more transparent about their production processes, ensuring that their workers are treated fairly and paid properly. A brand's ethical standards are becoming a crucial factor that shoppers consider when deciding where to spend their money.

4.6. The Challenge and Future of Conscious Consumerism

Despite the progressive shift towards more sustainable and ethical consumption patterns, the road ahead is not without its bumps. For instance, greenwashing has emerged as a significant issue where companies give a false impression of environmental responsibility. Consumers must remain vigilant to ensure their purchases are genuinely sustainable, not merely marketed as such.

Moreover, sustainable fashion often comes with a higher price tag due to the investment in quality materials and fair labor practices. Making sustainable fashion accessible to all strata of society is an ongoing challenge and an important goal for the future of the industry.

In conclusion, conscious consumerism has reshaped the fashion industry markedly, representing a significant step towards a more sustainable and fair global economy. This concept will continue to evolve, demanding even more significant changes. How the fashion industry will innovate while continuing to respect our environment and humanity is a thrilling prospect.

Chapter 5. Throwaway Culture: How Fast Fashion Feeds the Landfill

It's hard to resist the lure of wanderlust piqued by an array of high streets and online stores, luring in consumers with promises of on-trend, inexpensive garments. As our wardrobes bulge with this fashion bonanza, the unseen casualties are quickly forgotten. The gutters of our closets are choked with garments we no longer want, feed into a vicious cycle of rapid consumption, and direct disposal.

5.1. The Allure of Fast Fashion

Fast fashion won the hearts of many with its charm—trendy styles, renewed continually, offered at affordable prices. The catalytic rise of brands such as H&M, Zara, and Forever 21 marked the onset of this era—an epoch that glorified micro-seasons and thrived on a thirst for novelty. However, this haste to churn out new designs feeds an unsustainable cycle of wear and discard, creating an echo of emptiness even amidst the excess.

5.2. Behind the Scenes of Consumption

The core issue lies in our consumption behavior: an increasing demand for variety and a decreasing lifespan of a garment. A report from the Ellen MacArthur Foundation, a leading figure in the fight against waste, reveals that clothing utilization, or the average number of times a garment is worn before it ceases to be used, has decreased by 36% compared to 15 years ago. This behavior translates into staggering facts. Globally, customers miss out on $460 billion of value each year by throwing away clothes that they could continue to wear.

5.3. The Environmental Impact

This throwaway culture impacts our environment drastically. Approximately 85% of all textiles go to the dump each year. Added to the yearly production of 100 billion garments worldwide, one can infer the gargantuan pressure on natural resources. The cost exceeds just the wasted materials—a cocktail of dyes, bleaching agents, and other chemicals seep into our ecosystems from discards, poisoning rivers, soils, and ultimately, our own health.

5.4. Carbon Footprint of Fashion

Every step of the fashion production process contributes to our global carbon footprint. From the farming of raw materials, such as cotton, to the manufacture and transportation of the final product, energy consumption scales rapidly. The resultant carbon emissions rank the fashion industry as the second-largest polluter, trailing only behind the oil industry.

5.5. Microplastic Menace

With synthetic materials like polyester dominating the fashion scene, another alarming issue comes into light—the release of microplastics. Each wash of these synthetic textiles releases about 700,000 microscopic plastic particles. These minute pollutants eventually accumulate in oceans, add to the diet of marine life, and enter the human food chain, posing a serious and potential threat to health.

5.6. Deeper into Landfills

Fast fashion items are not designed for durability or longevity. As a result, they rarely catch the eye of second-hand markets. The majority of discarded clothing ends up in landfills, where synthetic fibers can take up to 200 years to decompose. Even natural materials, under anaerobic landfill conditions, produce potent greenhouse gases like methane during decomposition.

5.7. The Social Cost

Beyond the environmental aspect, fast fashion drags along a tale of human rights atrocities. From child labor to unsafe working conditions and unethically low wages, the glitter of affordable fashion often masks sorrowful tales from the sweatshops of developing nations.

In conclusion, while it's convenient to blame corporations for the surplus of throwaway fashion, the onus is not theirs alone. Our consumption choices shape market trends and, by extension, production practices. As conscious consumers, we must audit our wardrobes, favor quality over quantity, and foster repair, reuse, and recycle attitudes. We need to shun the idea of instantaneous disposal and instead, walk towards a future where styles endure, and fashion respects, rather than exploits, our planet. Fast fashion might have manipulated our perceptions of cost, value, and necessity, but it's not too late to rewrite the codes. It's time to rethink, reinvent, and refashion.

Chapter 6. Redefining Luxury in the Age of Sustainability

As the perception of luxury evolves together with the development of societal norms and shifts, the focus on sustainability has grown to be an essential aspect of perceived lavishness. No longer exclusively associated with opulence and extravagance, luxury now adopts a greener persona and high-end fashion is not an exception.

6.1. Unveiling Sustainability in Luxury Fashion

Sustainable luxury is now an integral part of the global wardrobe - an array of delectably unique items that harmoniously blend style with proactive measures towards sustainability. This is a far cry from traditional luxury that was equated with conspicuous consumption. Current luxury fashion is embedding sustainable practices into their operation — from sourcing, production, and distribution to customer engagement.

Traditional luxury brands, through their unique history and craftsmanship, have often been timeless. Yet, while these brands have a legacy of quality and longevity, environmental concerns were never at the forefront. However, as well noted, the 'throw-away' fashion is rapidly falling out of favour with consumers. Brands are adopting slow fashion, upcycling, and circular economy models to stay relevant: a nod to the fact that luxury can indeed embrace sustainability.

6.2. The Role of Consumers and their Evolving Tastes

Promoting sustainability within luxury fashion is more than a mere change in materials or manufacturing processes, crucially, it's driven by the consumers' evolving tastes. Following the increasing awareness of climate change and other environmental issues, consumers no longer view luxury fashion solely based on exclusiveness or costly materials. Instead, they appreciate brands that represent their values and echo their concerns about the environment. Thus, the new definition of luxury thrives on business models that value longevity, quality, and sustainability.

Weaving sustainability into their business strategies, brands enhance their appeal for eco-conscious consumers. Many luxury fashion brands are shifting towards an offering of ethically sourced and produced items, recycling programs, and even renewable energy in stores.

6.3. New Tech Transforming Luxury Fashion

What is intriguing about this phenomenon is the convergence of fashion and technology. Digital innovation in the fashion industry has led to not only novel materials but also new means of production. Fabrics from seaweed, mushroom leather, and other plant-based textiles look to replace high-impact materials like traditional leather and synthetic fibres.

Similarly, 3D printing promises additional efficiency in terms of resource consumption. Brands can utilise 3D printing to create garments to fit the exact dimensions of their customers, resulting in less material waste and a more personalised luxury experience.

Digital technology not only revolutionise the manufacturing side but also the retail experience. Blockchain, for example, offers consumers the chance to view the entire supply chain journey of their item, allowing them an insight that can ensure the ethical manufacturing they desire.

In the grand schema, these technological applications can help reduce waste and overproduction while delivering a superior, personalised product. A more streamlined, efficient process could lead to higher profit margins, representing a financial incentive for brands to consider sustainability in earnest.

6.4. The Challenges in Achieving Sustainable Luxury

While the marriage of luxury and sustainability appears harmonious, it is not without its challenges. For starters, there is a diversity issue on the sustainability front. Many of the clothes produced sustainably come in limited size ranges, which contributes to a divisive trend in sustainable fashion.

Moreover, transparency is far from ubiquitous throughout the industry. As marketing claims around sustainability become widespread, some consumers experience difficulty deciphering between brands truly invested in eco-friendly practices and those merely greenwashing their image.

Lastly, while the cost of sustainable practices and materials continues to decline, luxury items made sustainably are not always available to mass consumer markets due to price barriers.

6.5. Guiding the Future of Sustainable Luxury

In the global fight against climate change, the fashion industry must rise to the occasion. Luxury fashion's unique position to influence tastes and trends makes it a very relevant pivot point in the move towards environmental sustainability.

The transformation of luxury into a sustainable space will take a concerted effort from brands, consumers, policymakers, and investors. Brands will need to invest in research and development to create innovative processes and find alternatives to traditional high-impact materials.

Importantly, consumers must continue to demand sustainable practices and products from brands. Policymakers and investors can support this transition with regulations and funding that encourage sustainable practices and advancements.

Ultimately, the new definition of luxury finds its identity in a blend of style, quality, heritage, and most importantly, a passion for ensuring our world and future generations thrive. Each thread woven with care, each stitch carrying a pledge to our planet - this is the luxury we seek today. As history has proven, fashion often leads the way in societal shifts – we now look to it for guidance as we dress ourselves in sustainability.

Chapter 7. Fabrics of the Future: Bio-Materials and Recyclables

Until recently, fashion consumption has been driven by a constant influx of new styles and designs, leading to immense pressure on resources, significant waste creation, and a colossal ecological footprint. Fortunately, the industry has reached an inflection point with heightened consumer awareness catalysing key structural changes: enter the trailblazers dedicated to creating fabrics of the future. Two key strands of innovation frame the current industry transformation: the booming bio-material industry and the burgeoning field of recyclables.

7.1. The Dawn of Bio-Materials

Bio-materials, derived from living or once-living organisms, offer an astonishing array of unexpected and novel applications for the fashion industry. These materials are generally classified into two categories: plant-derived and animal-derived. Each offers its unique advantages and challenges.

Firstly, let's delve into the realm of plant-derived bio-materials. Cotton, arguably the most recognisable plant-based fabric, has been a staple in the fashion industry for centuries. However, the environmentally intensive cultivation methods required by cotton has led innovators to explore numerous other plant-based alternatives. Notable amongst these are hemp, flax, pineapple, banana, and even algae-based fabrics.

Hemp, for instance, is not only capable of producing fabrics with excellent durability but is also relatively easy to cultivate, requiring less water and yielding soil-enriching by-products. As public opinion around the cannabis Sativa plant is transformed, the hemp industry will likely continue to expand its green footprint. Flax, too, is gaining attention. The stiff fibers from the stalk of the plant are spun into a yarn used to create a high-quality linen highly appreciated for hot climates.

Perhaps most interesting are the fabrics derived from pineapple leaves and banana stems, i.e., Pinatex and Bananatex. These innovative materials rescue waste from the agricultural industry, offering a two-in-one solution for the environment. Algae, arguably one of the most versatile organisms on Earth, are also being tweaked and tested to create algae-derived fabrics with preliminary results indicating excellent dye retention and breathable builds.

Equally intriguing is the world of animal-derived bio-materials. Wool remains one of the most commonly employed animal-based fabrics due to its durability and insulation qualities. However, other lesser-known bio-materials are coming to light, such as Qmonos, a synthetic spider silk material that is eco-friendly and easier to produce. Even the beauty of a butterfly's wings is being harnessed with a unique biodegradable material created from chitosan, a substance derived from discarded crustacean shells.

Such bio-materials are revolutionising the way we think about fashion and are laying a sustainable path ahead. However, development and widespread adoption pose a significant barrier that needs to be overcome.

7.2. Spotlight on Recyclables

The second part of our path to a sustainable future lies in the intelligent use of recyclable materials. These materials, gleaned from our waste or cast-offs, are being resurrected and reincarnated into exciting new applications.

One of the most ubiquitous materials in this domain is recycled polyester or rPET. Made from recycled plastic bottles, rPET is becoming increasingly popular and is used in everything from sportswear to day-to-day fashion clothing. This fabric possesses the same properties as virgin polyester but with a far lesser environmental impact.

Additionally, a promising innovation lies in the recycling of discarded fishing nets. These nets are transformed into a nylon replacement known as Econyl. This new material is not only perfect for making swimwear and other clothing but its production also significantly helps marine life by reducing the quantity of discarded fishing gear.

Another up-and-coming innovation is the use of coffee grounds in fabric production. This technology transforms the ground coffee into yarn, creating a fabric with exceptional odour control properties, UV protection, and fast-drying capabilities.

Waste cotton, too, hasn't been neglect in the race for recyclable materials. Groundbreaking technology can mechanically recycle cotton by breaking down the fibres and re-spinning it, creating a fabric that avoids the environmental impact of growing and processing new cotton.

7.3. Challenges and the Future Ahead

As promising and enticing as these technologies sound, bio-materials and recyclables aren't devoid of hurdles. Generally, these revolve around issues of scalability, cost-effectiveness, awareness, and textile properties - including durability, feel, and care requirements. Profound research and development, as well as robust policy support, are necessary to help uplift these sustainable initiatives on a global scale.

From growers to manufacturers, and researchers to end consumers, every constituent of the fashion ecosystem has a crucial role to play in propelling this sartorial revolution forward. This comprehensive understanding, intertwining the past, present, and future of fabrics, is essential to building a wardrobe that's not only haute couture but also respects Mother Nature.

In the future, our sartorial choices will not be aligned just with trends, but with personal values too. The fashion industry as we know it is transforming, and we are privileged to witness and participate in this remarkable transition from unsustainable practices to environmentally-friendly ones.

The road to sustainable fashion is long and arduous, but the fabrics of the future illuminate the pathway. Powered by the promise of bio-materials and recyclables, we will walk that road, stitching the fabric of a better future as we go along. Let us strive to be conscientious consumers and advocate for these sustainable choices, weaving environmental advocacy into the very fabric of our lives.

Chapter 8. Zero-Waste Design: The Art of Sustainable Pattern-Making

As the fashion industry awakens to the harsh reality of its environmental damage, 'zero waste design' or 'ZWD' is emerging as a frontrunner remedy. Emphasizing the approach of 'no scrap left behind', collectively, we are propelling towards a system where not a single fibre is wasted. In this immersion into the ethos of zero-waste design, we explore the essence of sustainable pattern-making, its current adoption, and future implications.

8.1. The Essence of Zero-Waste Design

A refined yet disruptive response to the waste epidemic in fashion, zero-waste design is the practice of creating clothing in a way that leaves no scraps of unused fabric behind. It's a novel approach to pattern-making that roots itself in frugality and sustainability, investing in a future of fashion where waste becomes an oxymoron. Traditional pattern cutting techniques often result in 15-20% fabric waste per garment, and in a multi-billion dollar industry producing billions of items annually, that amount is catastrophic. On the contrary, zero-waste designs ensure that every inch counts.

8.2. Sustainable Pattern-Making: A New Learning Curve

At the heart of zero-waste design lies sustainable pattern-making, a process which requires intrinsic understanding of form and drape, and an unusual dedication to the minute details of tailoring. It's a meticulous yet creative process, grounded in trial and error, and innovation.

It calls for designers to think outside the traditional silhouette, re-envisioning how fabric interacts with the body. No longer must a sleeve be just a sleeve, but instead, become a versatile extension of the overall garment, cunningly designed to utilize every bit of material. Similarly, the garment's body can employ folds, pleats, tucks, and dart manipulation to avoid offcuts.

8.3. The Heroes of Zero Waste

In the space of ZWD, several designers worldwide have been instrumental in sowing the seeds of change. Designers such as Holly McQuillan, Timo Rissanen, and Tonlé have leveraged zero waste design to successfully create collections without compromising either style or sustainability.

Holly McQuillan, based in New Zealand, uses the ethos of Zero Waste in both her design practice and teaching. Her designs highlight an extraordinary blend of artistry and minimal waste, setting a precedent for future artisans.

Timo Rissanen, a New York-based designer, leads the revolution in a unique way by incorporating the concept of zero waste into education, thereby shaping how the next generation of designers approach fashion design patterns.

Tonlé, a fashion brand in Cambodia, is putting zero-waste design on a commercial scale, creating a model for other companies to follow. Their production process is an uncanny orchestra of a circular economy model, a remnant material sourcing strategy, and zero-waste pattern-making.

8.4. Future of Zero-Waste Design

The future of zero-waste design is an open-ended journey which beckons to be forged with collective efforts. It is essential to base future efforts on educating designers about the importance and techniques of zero-waste, advocating for transparency in the design process, and promoting recycling and upcycling initiatives.

It's a future where fashion reconciles with nature, harmony is navigated through creative solutions, and sustainability becomes an innate characteristic of the industry rather than an optional extra.

8.5. Challenges and Possible Solutions

While zero-waste design offers a promising reduction of fabric waste, it also presents challenges. The complexities and nuances of the design process can be time-consuming and require meticulous planning. Designers may feel restricted in their creative process, and commercially, zero-waste designs may command higher costs due to their labor-intensive nature.

However, by placing sustainability at the heart of fashion education, nurturing transparent supply chains, encouraging collaborative workspaces, and advocating technological advancements in sustainable pattern-making, we can navigate these challenges successfully.

In conclusion, zero-waste design is more than just a trend; it represents the dawn of a revolution in the fashion industry. A revolution that pledges to uproot the established norms of fashion production, to diminish waste at every step, and to march towards a sector where sustainability and style coexist effortlessly.

Chapter 9. Innovations in Supply Chain: Circular Economy as the Solution

As the fashion industry strides towards a more sustainable future, understanding the dynamics of supply chain transformation becomes pivotal. Central to this transformation lies the concept of a circular economy - a novel, regenerative approach that aims to eliminate waste, keep resources in use, and promote organic regrowth.

9.1. The Circular Economy: An Overview

The circular economy is a strategic response to today's linear 'take, make and dispose' economy which exploits resources without considering the environmental implications. The key principles underpinning a circular economy include designing out waste, keeping products and materials in use, and regenerating natural systems.

Instead of discarding resources after use, the circularity mandates the flow of resources to be circular. It moves beyond the traditional recycling measures and seeks to redesign, repurpose, restore, and regenerate.

9.2. Moving from Linear to Circular Supply Chains

Transitioning from linear to circular supply chains would entail a complete redesign of current practices. Start by evaluating each phase of the supply chain - from sourcing, design, and production to retail, consumption, and end-of-use management. Minimize resource usage in all stages while maximizing product life spans. This will demand innovative approaches like eco-design, zero-waste production, reverse logistics and heightened consumer awareness.

The fashion industry, in particular, will have to redefine raw material sourcing, opt for more sustainable fabrics that are biodegradable or easily recyclable, and explore novel technologies for efficient design and manufacturing.

9.3. Innovations in Material Sourcing

Circular supply chain starts with sustainable raw material sourcing. Innovation is rampant in this field, from organic cotton and hemp to novel materials like Pinatex - a natural leather substitute derived from pineapple cellulose, or Mylo - a fungus-based leather alternative.

Traditional materials like cotton, wool, and silk, when sourced organically, have less detrimental impact on the environment in terms of chemical usage, water consumption, and biodiversity loss. On the other hand, pioneering new materials provide fresh opportunities for fashion circularity, promising equal durability and style.

9.4. Adopting Eco-Design

'Eco-design' or 'sustainable design' promotes designing garments with their entire lifecycle in mind. This means considering every aspect from choice of material to the ease of disassembly at end-of-life. The goal is to minimize environmental impact while still delivering

Incorporating modularity in fashion design is one such innovation. Clothes constructed in a modular fashion can easily be taken apart. Thus, individual elements can be replaced rather than disposing of the whole item. This extends the garment's life, changing the whole perception of fashion from seasonal to timeless.

9.5. Production with Zero Waste

Zero-waste production aspires to eliminate all waste emanating during a garment's manufacturing process. Innovative design techniques, digital prototyping to minimize physical sampling, and efficient usage of cut pieces contribute to a waste-free production.

Moreover, technologies like 3D knitting that weave a garment in one go, without producing offcuts, are gaining traction. Such innovations are significantly reducing production waste while ensuring efficiency.

9.6. Reverse Logistics: Maximising the Value of Returns

Reverse logistics focuses on recovering as much value as possible from returned or discarded products. It involves collecting used products, extracting residual value through repair or reuse, and ensuring safe disposal of non-reusable or non-recyclable components.

Innovations like deposit-return schemes, online platforms for clothes exchanges, and brands accepting their old items back promote circularity. They not only offer value for end-to-use products but also help in cutting down fashion waste.

9.7. Building Consumer Awareness

The success of circular supply chains heavily banks on consumer participation. Brands are therefore required to educate consumers about the importance of responsible consumption and end-of-life management.

Initiatives like care and repair workshops, detailed care instructions, and awareness campaigns about the environmental consequences of fast fashion are progressively sensitizing consumers towards a more circular fashion culture.

The drive towards a sustainable future necessitates a substantial reshaping of the supply chains to become circular. As we open our eyes wider to the possibilities it presents, the fashion industry will continue to innovate, taking the monumental shift from a linear, exploitative model towards a circular, sustainable one.

Chapter 10. Financing Green Ventures: Unveiling the Role of Investors

In the realm of sustainable fashion, green ventures are the catalysts driving the industry forward towards a brighter, more eco-friendly future. However, these ventures cannot operate in a vacuum, necessitating the essential role of financial support. The investors supporting these enterprises are the unsung heroes, effectively paving the path to a sustainable future. Their understanding and provision of finance aid innovators to birth their sustainable ideas into reality and steer the industry towards transformation.

10.1. The Investor Landscape in Sustainable Fashion

The investor landscape in the sustainable fashion sector is a diverse one, ranging from venture capitalists to impact investors and crowdfunding platforms. Their varied funding sources provide the necessary financial fuel to power green ventures. Each class of investors offers a unique blend of resources and mentorship, proving instrumental to the rise and prospering of sustainable fashion start-ups. This diversified investor landscape has paved the way for various innovative, forward-thinking initiatives that look beyond simply making gains, instead focusing on a sustainable, profitable future.

Venture capitalists are traditionally characterised by their risk-taking nature, investing in start-ups with high growth potential. They offer substantial financial support to facilitate scale and expansion. Impact investors, on the other hand, are driven by the dual mandate of generating financial returns and social or environmental impact.

They typically seek out sustainable fashion start-ups that align with their mission. Lastly, crowdfunding platforms have grown in popularity, given their democratic nature of funding, allowing the wider public to pitch in and contribute to the growth of green ventures.

10.2. The Significance of Green Venture Financing

Green venture financing plays a pivotal role in moulding the future of sustainable fashion, acting as the key that unlocks the door to innovation and transformation. Without robust financial backing, even the most promising green venture can struggle to make a significant impact.

Market reach, product innovation, research and development, sustainability-oriented strategies, all require capital to be effectuated successfully. It is here that green venture financing steps in, providing the financial resources required to turn these concepts into reality, reinforcing the importance of adequate funding for sustainable fashion ventures.

10.3. Attracting Investments: A Balancing Act

Attracting investments for green ventures is not just about having a breakthrough product or an innovative idea. It's about striking the right balance between financial viability and environmental impact. Investors gauge start-ups on both these parameters before deciding to invest.

Green ventures must understand investor expectations, and craft their business models accordingly. A strong emphasis on sustainability, coupled with a sound financial strategy, proves to investors that the venture can generate both robust returns and impactful change.

10.4. The Investor's Role Beyond Finance

While financing is pivotal, the role of investors in sustainable fashion extends far beyond merely providing funds. They also serve as advisors, mentors, and industry connectors, facilitating the growth and development of green ventures from various perspectives.

Investors often share their seasoned expertise and industry knowledge, guiding green fashion enterprises through complex decisions and market dynamics. They facilitate networking and introduce start-ups to other like-minded businesses and veterans, often leading to fruitful collaborations and partnerships.

10.5. Navigating Challenges: Risks and Returns

Like all investments, green venture financing is not without risks. Market uncertainties, regulatory changes, or a failed product could all lead to a loss of investment. However, the rising global emphasis on sustainability, increasing consumer consciousness, and the sector's innovative resilience indicate that the potential for returns outweigh the risks involved.

Understanding these risks, and effectively mitigating them, is critical for attracting and retaining investors in the sustainable fashion sector. For this, businesses need to be transparent, realistic about their objectives and limitations, and constantly strive to build trust with their investors.

In conclusion, the role of investors in shaping the future of the sustainable fashion industry cannot be overstated. Their financial support drives the operational and creative aspects of green ventures, facilitating innovation, growth, and transformative change. Their influences are instrumental in making sustainable fashion not just a desirable concept, but an attainable and thriving reality. As the industry continues to evolve, the importance of green venture financing will only grow more pronounced, forging a future where sustainability and profitability coexist harmoniously in the world of fashion.

Chapter 11. Case Studies: Brands Leading the Sustainable Fashion Revolution

In the arena of sustainable fashion, a collection of brands stand out for their innovative, environmentally friendly practices. The following case studies delve into how these leaders are spearheading the environmentally-conscious revolution in the industry.

11.1. Stella McCartney

Known for her strong advocacy for animal rights and long-standing commitment to sustainability, Stella McCartney has forged a trailblazing path in luxury fashion. The brand's pillars are driven by sustainable sourcing, technological innovation and circular economy.

The Stella McCartney brand has championed the use of sustainable materials since its launch in 2001. For example, the brand uses organic cotton, responsibly sourced wool and regenerated cashmere. Recycled materials are also prioritized, with recycled polyester and nylon constituting 60% and 55% respectively of their material usage in 2020.

In addition to material innovations, transparency is woven into the brand's operation philosophy. Stella McCartney discloses their carbon, water, and waste footprint annually, showcasing their dedication to accountability on their sustainability journey.

11.2. Patagonia

Known for outdoor attire, Patagonia is a pioneer in the fight for sustainable fashion. The company adheres to the philosophy of 'build the best product, cause no unnecessary harm, use business to protect nature'. This ethos is echoed in their every strategy, driving them towards a circular business model.

Patagonia heavily invests in materials that are recyclable, restorable or biodegradable. Their notable "Worn Wear" initiative encourages customers to return used Patagonia items to be repaired and resold at a reduced price. Their innovative durability and repair programs significantly extend the lifespan of their products, reducing their overall environmental impact.

11.3. Eileen Fisher

What sets Eileen Fisher apart is their holistic approach towards sustainability. Their vision, "Where waste equals food", directs their journey to be 100% sustainable. They strive to use only organic cotton and linen, recycled fibres and responsibly-sourced wool.

A prominent initiative is their take-back program, "Renew", where used Eileen Fisher clothes are bought back, cleaned, mended and resold. Clothing beyond repair is artfully converted into one-of-a-kind pieces under their "Waste No More" project, contributing to a closed-loop system.

11.4. Veja

Veja is a trainer brand built around ecological concepts and fairness. Its sustainability commitments are embedded in their supply chain practices. By sourcing organic cotton directly from growers in Brazil, Veja ensures a fair price for farmers and reduces the use of harmful pesticides.

Veja's 'upcycle to cycle' policy relies on innovative materials, using a percentage of recycled cotton and plastic bottles to create new shoes. Transparency is another cornerstone of Veja. They publish a detailed account of their production processes and materials, including the impacts and challenges of implementing sustainable practices.

11.5. Reformation

The Los Angeles-based brand, Reformation, is renowned for chic, vintage-inspired clothing. Their sustainability mission revolves around being 'carbon, water and waste neutral'. To offset their CO2 emissions, they invest in projects that reduce greenhouse gases by the same amount.

All textiles used are sustainable, comprising surplus stock (deadstock), organic cotton, Tencel Lyocell and recycled materials. They have a 'RefRecycling' program where customers can send back Reformation or other brand clothes to be recycled.

Reformation believes in radical transparency. They publish 'RefScale', tracking their environmental footprint per product, teaching consumers about the impacts of their purchases.

The case studies mentioned above showcase the diverse ways global fashion brands are leading the sustainable revolution. From raw material sourcing to manufacturing processes, each company has a unique approach to reducing environmental impact, fostering social responsibility, and driving the industry forward toward a sustainable future.